Steve Kerr: The Inspiring Life and Leadership Lessons of One of Basketball's Greatest Coaches

An Unauthorized Biography & Leadership Case Study

By: Clayton Geoffreys

Visit my website at www.claytongeoffreys.com
Cover photo by Keith Allison is licensed under CC BY 2.0 / modified from original

Table of Contents

Foreword

Few former players and color commentators have made as seamless of a transition to becoming the head coach of an NBA team as Steve Kerr. Since being hired to replace Mark Jackson in the summer of 2014, the Warriors have entered a golden period of playing at the highest level of excellence. At the time of this writing, the Warriors are crusading through their third consecutive NBA Finals appearance, with the opportunity to seize another championship to add to their 2015 title. Kerr's talent and skill as a head coach was not something that came overnight. It took years of studying as a player playing for some of the industry's greatest such as Phil Jackson, to learning under arguably the greatest coach of the modern era, Gregg Popovich. Kerr contains many of the traits that make an effective leader. He devotes a great deal of preparation towards his day to day, always approaches problems with a learner's mindset, and stays humble despite his great successes. Thank you for purchasing

Steve Kerr: The Inspiring Life and Leadership Lessons of One of Basketball's Greatest Coaches.

In this unauthorized biography and leadership case study, we will learn some of the background behind Steve Kerr's incredible life story, and more importantly his impact on the game of basketball. In the last section of the book, we'll learn what makes Steve Kerr such an effective leader and coach, including a review of key takeaways that you can remember when looking to apply lessons from Steve Kerr to your own life. Hope you enjoy and if you do, please do not forget to leave a review!

Also, check out my website at claytongeoffreys.com to join my exclusive list where I let you know about my latest books. To thank you for your purchase, you can go to my site to download a free copy of *33 Life Lessons: Success Principles, Career Advice & Habits of Successful People.* In the book, you'll learn from some of the greatest thought leaders of different industries on what it takes to become successful and how to live a great life.

Cheers,

Clayton Geoffreys

Visit me at www.claytongeoffreys.com

Introduction

Rarely do NBA head coaches immediately make an impact in the league where all the greatest minds in basketball coach the best athletes of the sport. It takes months or even years to try to convince the players and entire organization to buy into the system you seek to sell. It would take even longer to perfect that system while several other teams in the league are brandishing strategies and plays they have been using for several years already.

What is even more difficult is to try to lead a young team that has minimal playoff experience on your first stint as a coach at any level of basketball. But the Golden State Warriors' Steve Kerr did it. He immediately made an impact in a league that already had established title favorites coming into his first season as a head coach of the Warriors. He would shake the heads of contenders, critics, and fans alike by leading a young and inexperienced Golden State

Warriors to a remarkable 67-15 regular season record and an eventual NBA title in his first season.

It was a perfect marriage of inexperience for both Steve Kerr and the Golden State Warriors during the 2014-15 season. The Golden State Warriors were off from one of their best seasons in recent memory after having reached the playoffs and putting up a good fight against the San Antonio Spurs, who would win the 2014 NBA championship, in the second round of the playoffs. Under then-head coach Mark Jackson, the Warriors experienced a type of success unseen before from a team that had struggled mightily since the 90's. But the Warriors had been improving under Jackson and were seen as a team that would go on to be contenders in the future under their then-head coach's leadership.

But Mark Jackson had a misunderstanding with ownership and management. It ultimately led to his departure from the Golden State Warriors, who everyone thought were back to square one after losing the coach that had led them back to relevance in the NBA. Nobody even thought that Steve Kerr, who was named the new head coach of the team, would make much of a difference considering that the Warriors had been successful under Jackson and that Kerr never had any experience coaching a team at any level.

Despite having no experience as a coach at any level of basketball, Steve Kerr was not an ordinary rookie strategist. For some of the best seasons of his career as a professional basketball player, Kerr played under the legendary Phil Jackson and his famed Triangle Offense when he was with the Chicago Bulls in the 90's. Steve Kerr would play a supportive role in a powerhouse team that featured Michael Jordan and Scottie Pippen. He would have several memorable clutch moments when he won three straight titles as a player with the Bulls, but it was his experience as a student of Phil Jackson that ultimately contributed to his future as a head coach.

After leaving the Chicago Bulls in 1998, Steve Kerr would again play under the tutelage of another all-time great strategist. At that time, the San Antonio Spurs' Gregg Popovich was still a novice as a head coach. Despite that, he was arguably one of the best minds in basketball. Kerr would learn the ins and outs of Pop's mindset as a coach in the three years he spent with the Spurs. He would win a title in his first year in San Antonio and then another one in 2003 in his final season as an NBA player.

Using his vast experience as a celebrated role player and one of the brightest minds that had played under the two best coaches of that era of basketball, Steve Kerr would take his talents to television broadcasting to work as an analyst for Turner Television Network (TNT) during live basketball games. He would spend four years with TNT as a color commentator beside the legendary Marv Albert for four years.

After his stint as a commentator, Kerr would move on to become the President and General Manager of the Phoenix Suns in 2007. He would be responsible for turning what was then thought of as a dying and aging Suns team into contenders in 2010. The Suns, who were famous for their run-and-gun offense, actually played good defense that season thanks partly to how Kerr traded for pieces that could make them a better defensive unit. They would push the eventual champions the Los Angeles Lakers into a hard-fought six-game series. Kerr would step down after that season and would return to work as a color commentator for TNT for another four years.

It was in 2014 when Steve Kerr was named the successor to Mark Jackson's Golden State Warriors. By that time, though it was his first time as a coach, be it as a lead or assistant, Kerr had already learned enough from his playing days and years as an analyst and front office executive. All of those experiences worked to his advantage.

Luckily for Kerr, he already had the pieces set. The Warriors were sporting the two best shooters in basketball. Stephen Curry and Klay Thompson were widely regarded as the best shooting duo in league history. He also inherited former All-Stars and key pieces in Andre Iguodala and David Lee. They also had youngsters Harrison Barnes and Draymond Green waiting in the wings for their breakout year.

Steve Kerr would take out everything he learned from the two great coaches and his stint as a General Manager. When he began coaching the team in the 2014 Summer League, elements of the Triangle Offense were evident. He used the post passing skills of David Lee and the shooting abilities of his guards to make sure there was always a triangle between the post player and perimeter guys. But he never stuck too much with the triangle offense considering that Kerr also used the pace-and-space style of Gregg Popovich to make a hybrid between Jackson's system and that of Pop's. And when there were transition opportunities,

Kerr made sure his team was running and gunning ala the Phoenix Suns of 2010.

When the regular season started, Steve Kerr and his Golden State Warriors became the surprising squad. Using the hybrid team-based offense he learned under Jackson and Popovich, Kerr had turned the Warriors into the best offensive unit the league had ever seen. And by utilizing the defensive capabilities of guys like Andrew Bogut, Harrison Barnes, Andre Iguodala, and the much-improved Draymond Green, the team had also become a surprisingly good defensive squad. Kerr would eventually break records as a rookie head coach on his way to a 67-15 campaign. He would then lead the Warriors to a 4-2 win over the Cleveland Cavaliers in the 2015 NBA Finals to become the first rookie head coach to win a title since Pat Riley did it in 1982.

While Steve Kerr may have won the title with strategy and tactics, what stood out in his first season as a head coach was his leadership. The Warriors had a young core, but also had key veteran pieces. Kerr instilled into Curry and Thompson the confidence that the best shooting duo in league history needed for a title run. He convinced Andre Iguodala and David Lee, who were both good enough to become All-Stars as leading men in other teams, to take bench roles for the greater good of the Warriors. He then allowed Draymond Green to transform himself into the all-around defensive beast that he eventually became.

Steve Kerr might have inherited a team that only needed the right push to become championship contenders, but it was the way he made the players buy into his system and into his leadership that made the Warriors the powerhouse team that they are. With his happy-go-lucky style and calm, laidback demeanor, Kerr allowed his players to be themselves and have fun on the court while managing egos that were in danger of getting out of hand. With that kind of a leadership style, Steve Kerr would then break the record for most wins in a regular season. He was part of the team that did it back in 1996 when he played for the Bulls, who won 72 regular season games. He then led the Warriors as the head coach when they finished the 2015-16 season with a 73-9 regular season record.

But while Steve Kerr and the Warriors fell within a game short of winning a consecutive NBA title in 2016, the future looks bright for the team. They acquired four-time scoring champion Kevin Durant during the offseason to form what is arguably the most potent offensive team in the history of the NBA. Marching in as title favorites in the 2017 playoffs, Steve Kerr's ability to lead and adjust his system to his players is what ultimately led the Warriors to become the powerhouse squad that they are today.

Chapter 1: Background and History

Steve Kerr's brilliant and strategic mind stems from a family line of academic leaders. His grandfather Stanley Kerr was an American humanitarian who spent most of his life in the field of biochemistry. He also spent a good part of his career as a biochemist as a professor. However, he would soon leave his job to pursue volunteer work in the Middle East, particularly in Aleppo during the Armenian Genocide. He would spend most of his time in the Middle East in Beirut, Lebanon as chairman of the Department of Biochemistry at the American University of Beirut.

Steven's father Malcolm would follow in Stanley's footsteps as an academic. He would specialize in Middle Eastern studies as he was born in Beirut and was raised there for a good part of his early life before he left for the United States for high school and college. He then spent time as a professor at the University of California-Los Angeles (UCLA) before relocating back to Beirut to become the President of the American University of Beirut (AUB) where he served as a professor in political science before the civil war broke out.

On September 27, 1965, Steve Kerr was born to Malcolm and Ann Kerr. At that time, Steve spent most of his childhood years in Lebanon when his father was still an assistant professor for the AUB. The family then later relocated back to California when Malcolm was offered a position to teach at UCLA. Malcolm would spend 20 years with UCLA before returning to the Middle East. Steve Kerr would spend his formative years growing up in Pacific Palisades, California.[i] He would attend high school at Palisades High in Los Angeles, where he played basketball as a guard that specialized from the outside.

Much of Steve Kerr's early years in Palisades were spent in the Kerr family driveway. Malcolm had installed a hoop above the family home's garage. He understood more than anyone that sports were a part of a race's culture just as any other tradition was. Sports were not merely an escape, but were rather a way of experiencing culture because different races tend to play certain styles depending on the way they were raised by their tradition.[ii]

But it was not all about basketball for Steve Kerr when he was a young boy. He spent most of his childhood and high school years hearing about his father raving news about peace developments in the Middle East. Ushering a peaceful era in that part of the world was always Malcolm Kerr's dream. It was one passed down by Stanley to his son. And while Steve may not have followed the same road as his father and grandfather did before him, he would forge a path towards relevance.

In the latter part of Steve Kerr's high school life, Malcolm was named to his dream job as president of the AUB. There were several reasons for Malcolm to stay in the US. The acting president of the AUB was recently kidnapped. Conflicts were happening even on the AUB campus. AUB even had to keep Malcolm out of Beirut and had him stay in New York for a while as the dust was settling in Lebanon. But he would eventually accept the job and fly over to Lebanon knowing very well the dangers that awaited him.[ii]

At that time, Steve Kerr was a senior at Palisades High. It was the first season for him to start as a guard. He even starred for the team back then. But the one thing he sorely wished for was for his father to see him playing and leading the team. His father was always a leader in his field. Malcolm was one of the leading Middle Eastern studies experts in the world. He was a leader in ushering peace in the Middle East. Stanley was the same. Stanley led a group of volunteers in helping Middle Eastern refugees.

While Steve was leading elsewhere and on another playing field, he was a leader nonetheless. It was always in the Kerr family's bloodline to lead. Stanley led, Malcolm led, and Steve would eventually become a leader in his right in a different and more peaceful war—a battle on the hardwood floor. It was his leadership skills that had him standing out in high school. But as far as basketball was concerned, all he could do was shoot.

With a high school career that was not stellar compared to other big name guards coming elsewhere, Steve Kerr was not a hot recruit coming out of Palisades. No other Division I school was interested in him. He had little to no athletic skills. He was a shooter—a great one at that. But that was the best and only thing unique about him as far as basketball skills were concerned.

Nevertheless, the University of Arizona took a chance with the guard born in Lebanon. At that time, the University of Arizona was not even the popular basketball hub that it is today. During his first few games with the Wildcats, he struggled to keep up with the more athletic players. And yet Steve Kerr made use of whatever opportunity he was given at Arizona.[ii]

But Steve Kerr almost never made it to Arizona to play for their basketball team. The summer before leaving for the University of Arizona for college, he had spent time in Beirut to visit his family amidst the turmoil in that part of the world. The Kerr household resided in the presidential house on the campus. Steve was the only one staying in the United States. Before he was about to leave, Beirut became a hotbed for attacks and bombings. Ann would immediately find a way to get her son out of Lebanon and on his way to Arizona, where he would have a bright future as a basketball player.[ii]

Malcolm would not be around to see Steve Kerr playing his first game for Arizona. However, he did receive a videotape of the event. Steve would score three baskets that night to the delight of his father, who was watching the tape halfway around the world. Though the footage was fuzzy and was taken far up in the stands, Malcolm knew who and where Steve was on the floor. Sadly, he would never have a chance to watch his son play for the University of Arizona in person.

On January 18, 1984, on the AUB campus, Malcolm Kerr would make his way to the office after stepping outside the elevator. Unexpectedly, two unknown assailants shot him in the back of his head twice to make sure their target would not walk out alive. The deed was committed by a group of Islamic extremist and Jihadists called the Islamic Holy War. The group resented the presence of Americans in Lebanon. What better way to make their intents known by assassinating the president of the American University of Beirut?[ii]

Steve Kerr would receive the hard-hitting news halfway around the world in the wee hours after midnight. It was from a family friend who phoned him in his freshman dorm at Arizona. With his world crashing down on him, Steve did not know what else to do. He would go outside of the dorm and run his feelings away crying as he did it.[iii]

Luckily for Steve Kerr, he had an outlet. He did not know what to do with the feelings of devastation engulfing him. He used basketball as an escape. The day after hearing the news, Steve would come to practice like nothing had happened. He even played for the team's next game. The team would play against Arizona State, the University of Arizona's bitter rivals.

The news about Malcolm Kerr's assassination was a national sensation. Everyone knew about it. Friends and teammates sympathized with Steve. They knew how the Arizona guard felt about the situation, but others were brutal and insensitive. In what would become a blowout victory, Steve Kerr would play out of his mind after hearing taunts from students from the opposing team. He almost never made it out of the locker room after tears started rolling out of his eyes a few minutes before tipoff. But he came out smoking off the bench by making his first three shots. He would lead the University of Arizona to win eight of their final 14 games after a dismal 2-11 start to the season. Kerr used his father's death as fuel for his inspired performances.[ii] Steve Kerr would average 7.1 points that season as a freshman.

The following year, Steve Kerr would play more minutes and would even start for the University of Arizona Wildcats. He was an avid fan favorite because of his ability to hit the jump shot with so much efficiency. It seemed so natural for him to hit shots from the perimeter. The better part of his game was that he picked his shots. Kerr knew when and from where to shoot. He was not the type that would simply jack up shots from the floor. Steve would average 10 points and four assists that season. Remarkably, he shot nearly 57% from the floor and led the Wildcats to an NCAA Tournament appearance. That was the start of the University of Arizona's dominance as a collegiate powerhouse.

Shortly after averaging 14.4 points, 4.2 assists, and 1.6 steals in his junior year with the Wildcats, Steve Kerr was named a member of the USA Basketball Team that would play in the FIBA World Championships in Spain. He was part of the last team of amateur players before the USA started to send professional players to world championship tournaments. But Kerr would eventually suffer and injury that season and would redshirt in what would have been his senior year at the University of Arizona. Nevertheless, he went home with a gold medal around his neck.

Rather than trying his hand at the NBA Draft, Steve Kerr returned the following year as a senior. He reprised his role as the crowd darling by hitting jumper after jumper. He even averaged 57.3% from the three-point area while norming 12.6 points and 3.9 assists in his final year with the Wildcats. He was then an integral member when the team made it all the way to the Final Four of the NCAA Tournament. That year, he also set an NCAA record for most three-pointers made in a single season. He also became the Wildcats' all-time leader in three-point shooting percentage.

But the most memorable part of Steve Kerr's final year with the University of Arizona was another brutal game against Arizona State. Rabid fans began jeering him about his father's death. They taunted him and even went as far as insulting him about Malcolm's untimely and unfortunate demise. A teary and emotional Steve Kerr responded by draining six three-pointers in the first half alone in what became a blowout win for the Wildcats.

While hard work and dedication to his craft were what made Steve Kerr a remarkable marksman in college, it was Malcolm's death that transformed him into the man he is today. Back in college, he already had the makings of a future coach. Steve was a great leader that treated his team like family. He was thousands of miles away from his family in Beirut, but he had another one in Arizona.[iv]

His personality was also his teammates' favorite part about him. Steve Kerr was just oozing with personality and a sense of humor. He did not lead with his numbers or with his abilities on the floor but was leading the team with the way he was getting the best out of his teammates. He helped his teammates reach their potential by expecting them to get better and better every single day. He treated everyone with respect as if they were a part of his family. That was a part of Steve Kerr that sparked predictions of his future role as a head coach in the NBA. But as of that moment, he had to make it to the big leagues first.

Chapter 2: NBA Career

The Early Years

Despite having a successful career in college mainly as a shooter and leader, Steve Kerr almost never made it to the NBA with his credentials. He was only a shooter. At that time, the league was not putting the same premium on shooters as they do today. Steve would only make it to the league by getting drafted in the second round. He was the 50th overall pick by the Phoenix Suns. But Steve Kerr's stint with Phoenix was short-lived. He would only play 26 games during his rookie season and would average only 2.1 points in 6 minutes a night.

The following season, he was traded to the Cleveland Cavaliers where he played backup to an all-time great point guard in Mark Price. When Price and Kerr were both on the floor, the Cavs had a pair of good shooters from the outside to strike daggers into the hearts of their opponents. Kerr would average 6.7 points and 3.2 assists in his first season with the Cavs.

A year later, Steve Kerr would see fewer minutes on the floor and would only play 57 games for the Cleveland Cavaliers. The next season, the trend was the same. Kerr was a role player who was merely called upon whenever the coach needed a shooter on the floor. Though Kerr played a limited role, he was one of the better backup guards in the league because of his ability to stretch the floor. The best part was that coaches had no ego to deal with when it came to him.

During the 1992-93 season, Steve Kerr was traded to the Orlando Magic after five games with the Cavs, where he spent the last three years with. His role was even worse in Orlando. He played less than 10 minutes a game and would only appear in 47 outings. Needless to say, Orlando did not have any use for him as a player or even as a floor leader.

Joining the Chicago Bulls, Learning Under Phil Jackson

Steve Kerr was a free agent after that stagnant season with the Orlando Magic. During the offseason, he would sign with a Chicago Bulls team that had just won their third consecutive NBA title under head coach Phil Jackson. But the problem was that the three-time Finals MVP and the man regarded as the best player on the planet had just left the team. Michael Jordan retired early in his career for personal reasons after the death of his father. The Bulls were leaning on a core trio of Scottie Pippen, Horace Grant, and BJ Armstrong.

But Steve Kerr almost never made it to the Chicago Bulls, let alone another NBA team after five seasons. Nobody even expected him to stay in the NBA that long. His year with the Orlando Magic was what made it clear that Steve Kerr did not belong to the big league. It seemed that Kerr was well on his way to a career outside of the NBA. He had taken a year of grad school at the University of Arizona. He would have gone back there and might have even joined the coaching staff, but he was given a tryout with the Bulls. In that day and age, NBA players did not walk into teams for tryouts. Teams sought out players, not the other way around.[v]

Steve took a chance with what was essentially a tryout for a non-guaranteed roster spot with the Chicago Bulls. After that, he was signed to a minimum one-year contract, which was not even guaranteed. The Bulls took him in because he could shoot and play either guard spot, but that was it. He was an insurance policy in case the other guards were not healthy. But the good part was that Phil Jackson liked his work ethic and the personality he brought to the floor.

Even without Michael Jordan, the 1993-94 Chicago Bulls were a competitive team that season because of the Triangle Offense system that Phil Jackson had perfected with the team. Jackson had his players running the Triangle even without the best player on the planet anchoring it. The system was so ingrained with the team that they could run it in their sleep. It was through the Triangle that Steve Kerr's worth was highlighted.

Steve Kerr immediately learned and adjusted to the ins and outs of the Triangle Offense. His role in the system was simple. He was out there as one of the three perimeter players as an option for the post player to pass to. He was always one of the three points of the triangle because of his ability to shoot. If not shooting, Kerr was intelligent enough to know where to pass the ball to when defenses recovered to him.

But what Kerr picked up from Jackson was not the system, nor the way Phil Jackson would chant incantations and spread incense around the locker room. Phil was made famous by his "Zen" ways. He approached coaching with a spiritual sense of sorts. He would have his players undergo Zen meditations and make them do yoga. Kerr had to experience all of those spiritual exercises but primarily picked up the intellectual part of Jackson's philosophy.

Steve Kerr saw how Phil Jackson approached the game. Jackson was always calm and reserved during practices and games. He was never too worried or concerned about the status of the game. He was the type of man that would not even call a timeout when the opposing team was on a run. Instead, he let his players figure the situation out themselves without pressing the panic button. This was a trait that Kerr learned to carry alongside many other qualities. He began learning more about the game from Jackson. He picked up Phil's ability to openly communicate with players and teammates. As a player, Steve Kerr was well on his way to become the next Phil Jackson of sorts.[vi]

Steve Kerr would spend the first two seasons with the Bulls as an integral part of the line-up. The roster was good, and it was good enough for some of the top playoff spots in the East. But they could not get over the hump in those first two years until Michael Jordan came back for a full 82-game campaign during the 1995-1996 season.

A then 30-year-old Steve Kerr was already a veteran of the NBA game. He had absorbed Phil Jackson's Triangle Offense and had become an important part of the rotation. Off the bench, he was tasked to play off the attention that Michael Jordan and Scottie Pippen got from the opposing defense. He played within the system while making sure the two all-time greats found him for open shots. The team was assembled so well that no other squad in the league could stop them. The Chicago Bulls ended up breaking a record for the most regular-season wins. At 72-10, they were the favorites to win the NBA title, which they eventually did against the Seattle SuperSonics in six games. That was Steve Kerr's first taste of being an NBA champion. In other news, he also led the league in three-point percentage by shooting over 50% from that distance.

The following season, the Chicago Bulls maintained their dominance over the entire NBA landscape. Everybody on the team had defined roles. Michael Jordan was Batman while Scottie Pippen was Robin. They had a bunch of Alfreds that would deliver big when they were needed. Steve Kerr was one of them. His marksmanship from the perimeter was a key weapon for the Chicago Bulls, who were only three wins short of their pace a season before.

Steve Kerr's ability to hit the jumpshot was never as important as it was in the dying seconds of Game 6 of the 1997 NBA Finals. The Chicago Bulls were up 3-2 in the series against the Utah Jazz led by Karl Malone and John Stockton, who are two of the all-time greats at their respective positions. With 25 seconds left to go and the game tied at 86-86, the Bulls called timeout.

During the huddle, the play was naturally called for Michael Jordan. But Jordan knew he was going to be ganged up on. During the huddle, he was sitting beside Kerr. He told the guard that he was going to pass him the ball and that he better be ready to shoot it. Kerr was more than ready. The hardships and experiences he had gone through had prepared him for that moment.[vi]

When play resumed, the ball found its way to Michael Jordan, who dribbled the ball all the way to the left wing from the top of the key. He attracted the defensive attention everybody knew he would be getting in those kinds of situations. John Stockton went in to double him to leave Steve Kerr open at the right wing. Kerr saw that Mike was in trouble and ran into position just two feet above the free throw line. Kerr received the pass and immediately rose up to shoot the ball with Stockton stumbling to recover over to him. Steve Kerr was the unlikely hero of the series after hitting the shot that would win the game and championship for the Chicago Bulls.

During the Bulls' victory parade, Steve Kerr showed the extraordinary sense of humor he was always been loved for. Telling his story about the shot, he jokingly said that Michael Jordan was not comfortable in those clutch situations and asked Phil Jackson himself to go to Steve Kerr. Kerr again jokingly stated that he was on his way to bailing out Michael Jordan once more after carrying him the entire season. The crowd and the entire Chicago Bulls team would show their love for Steve by laughing at his story. That kind of a personality and willingness to step up was what made Steve Kerr one of the most adored figures in the entire NBA.

The following season, Kerr reprised his role as the Chicago Bulls' top gunner from the three-point line. Again, he would not start a single game, but would nonetheless play the integral role he had always been

35

asked to do. He helped the Bulls win title number six and secure another three-peat in a span of eight seasons. The then 32-year-old three-time champion had done all he could for the Bulls. And just like Michael Jordan and Phil Jackson did after that season, he would leave Chicago to move on elsewhere.

Learning Under Pop, Winning with the Spurs

Phil Jackson would move on to coach the Los Angeles Lakers for the 1998-99 season. Meanwhile, Steve Kerr would get traded to the San Antonio Spurs in exchange for a first-round draft pick. In San Antonio, Steve Kerr would have a chance to gun for a fourth straight NBA title given that the Spurs were the most dominant team in the league just a season after Jordan retired. They were banking on the all-time great talents of Tim Duncan and David Robinson, who led the Spurs to a 37-13 record in a shortened regular season. But the most important part of Kerr's stop in San Antonio was how he learned under Gregg Popovich.

At that time, Gregg Popovich was still untested as an NBA head coach. He had just taken over the San Antonio Spurs two seasons ago when the team was in turmoil because of Robinson's injury. Before taking over as head coach, Pop never had experience in that role except for when he coached a Division III school back in the 80's. In the NBA, he spent most of his time as an assistant to Larry Brown before he was given the post as the Spurs' General Manager during the mid-90's.

Despite Pop's inexperience as a head coach in the NBA, he was already one of the brightest minds in the league. He had studied and learned under Mike Brown and was always one of the few coaches that loved thinking outside the box. He never constrained himself to one single system or to a trend that seemed successful for other teams. Other than being a bright mind, Gregg Popovich was also a caring leader that treated his players and coaching staff like family. He was, in many ways, like Steve Kerr. They both had a good sense of humor and treated everyone in the organization with respect worthy of a family member. Pop was an ideal mentor for someone like Steve Kerr.

The beauty about Gregg Popovich as a head coach was that he had no clear-cut system. The Spurs played a slow pace on offense. They would pound the ball inside the paint where both Duncan and Robinson dominated with their size advantage. It was an offense anchored on the team's big men. Nevertheless, Pop always preached ball movement. He never liked relying on one player alone. Even when Duncan and Robinson were not on the floor, the Spurs could still function just as well as if the twin tower duo were not on the bench. While Popovich loved putting an emphasis on sharing the ball on offense, the Spurs were more famous for a defense that funneled guards towards the big men inside.

As a vital part of the Spurs' rotation, Steve Kerr was the beneficiary of the defensive attention that the twin towers were getting inside. He was getting open looks from the perimeter, though he was shooting low percentages from the three-point range in his first season with San Antonio. At that point, Gregg Popovich tried to shy away from letting his players shoot the three ball. Nevertheless, he saw Steve Kerr as a valuable piece because of his leadership and timely shots from the outside. It would not take long for Kerr to win a fourth consecutive NBA title that season as a member of the Spurs.

Steve Kerr would spend two more seasons with the San Antonio Spurs, but would end up losing almost every season to the Los Angeles Lakers of Phil Jackson in the playoffs. During those seasons, age had already gotten to Steve Kerr, who was mainly used for his outside shooting. As good of a leader and shooter that he was, Popovich would say that Kerr could not play defense even if he tried. Nevertheless, he still found himself playing for the Portland Trailblazers for one season before returning to the Spurs during the 2002-03 campaign.

In what would be his final year in the NBA, Steve Kerr was already 37 years old and was playing a minimal role. His best role for the team was being a mentor to young guards Tony Parker and Manu Ginobili. However, he did find himself contributing big in a hard-fought Western Conference battle against the Dallas Mavericks in the Conference Finals. In Game 6, he would help key a win and elimination by hitting four three-pointers in the second half alone, though three-point shooting was not a forte of the Spurs. San Antonio would eventually earn a title that season. It was Kerr's fifth overall championship ring in the 15 seasons he spent with the NBA. He would retire averaging only 6 points, but his 45.4% shooting clip from the three-point area remains to be a record in the NBA up to now.

Chapter 3: Life After the NBA

The Broadcaster

Steve Kerr would immediately begin a career as a broadcaster for TNT's coverage of the NBA games after he retired from the game. Kerr would initially spend four years with Turner before working as an executive for the Phoenix Suns in 2007. He would return in 2010 to work for four more years as a broadcaster before eventually leaving to coach the Golden State Warriors.

As a television analyst, Steve Kerr was often lauded for his soft-spoken voice and knowledge about the game of basketball. Such knowledge spanned from his experience playing with the likes of Michael Jordan and Scottie Pippen and under the tutelage of Phil Jackson in his first three titles with the Chicago Bulls before he would go on to win two more rings with the San Antonio Spurs under the watchful eye of Gregg Popovich.

What made Steve Kerr a beloved broadcast analyst in the eight years he spent doing the job was not his voice or catchphrases. Kerr always had an eye for observing plays. Some analysts would rave about the thunderous dunk or the dagger three-pointer. Meanwhile, Steve Kerr would talk about the sequences and passes that led to those dunks and three-pointers.

Spending time with Michael Jordan, Scottie Pippen, and Dennis Rodman, who are three of the greatest defenders at their respective positions, also helped Kerr understand the ins and outs of players' ability to defend. And the years he spent under Pop, whose defensive strategies were second to none during those dominant seasons, were invaluable in helping Kerr explain how team defenses work during live broadcasts.[vii]

The Executive

Between his broadcast years with TNT, Steve Kerr would spend three seasons as the General Manager of the Phoenix Suns, the very same team that drafted him 50th overall back in 1988. At that time, Kerr was one of the owners of the Phoenix Suns. And when he was still a broadcaster, he worked as part of the Suns' management group.

In 2007, he would effectively assume the role of the Phoenix Suns' General Manager. While the Suns were competing well with their run-and-gun offense the past few years, Kerr felt that the team was too small and weak on the defensive end to contend with the likes of the Spurs and Lakers during the postseason. He would then orchestrate a controversial trade that sent fan favorite Shawn Marion to the Miami Heat in exchange for an aging Shaquille O'Neal. Though Phoenix made the playoffs, they were bested by the Spurs in the first round in only five games.

The following season, Steve Kerr would hire Terry Porter as the new head coach after former head coach Mike D'Antoni left and decided to go to New York.

Porter would try to change the Suns' style into a slow-paced offense that relied on defense. In the middle of all that, Kerr would also trade for Jason Richardson and Jared Dudley to effectively remake the roster leaving only Steve Nash and Amar'e Stoudemire as the remaining players of the run-and-gun Suns era.

Unfortunately, the experiment with Porter failed. In the middle of the season, management would fire Terry Porter and replace him with Alvin Gentry, who brought back the run-and-gun style but used some of Porter's defensive schemes to form a Suns team that could score in a hurry while also defending well on the other end. However, Phoenix failed to make the postseason that year.

Before the 2009-10 season in what would become Steve Kerr's final campaign as GM of the Suns, the future head coach would trade away Shaquille O'Neal for Ben Wallace and a package of draft picks to bring back the running game of Phoenix. The Suns would make it all the way to the Western Conference Finals that season before bowing out to the Lakers in six games.

While Steve Kerr's first season as GM was marred with criticisms considering that he almost ran the Suns to the ground, the moves he made eventually paid off. Trading for Jason Richardson and Jared Dudley allowed Phoenix to gain two respectable shooters. Richardson was a good scorer in his right while Dudley could shoot the three ball and defend the perimeter well. They were both key pieces in helping the Suns make it to the Conference Finals in 2010.

Some of Steve Kerr's draft picks during his run as GM were also key for the Suns' future. In 2008, he drafted Robin Lopez in the first round. Lopez turned out to be one of the best defensive big men in the league for his price tag. Kerr also drafted Goran Dragić back then. Dragić would turn into an All-Star at one point in his career.

Though it was not the best run for him as an executive, Steve Kerr did well enough to set up the Suns for the future. He would step down in 2010 as President and GM of the Suns, but still kept his share with the team until 2014. He returned to his former duty as a broadcaster for four more years before he was fatefully called upon to become the head coach of the Golden State Warriors.

Chapter 4: Head Coaching Career

The Rookie Champion Coach

Before the 2014-15 season got underway, former Chicago Bulls and Los Angeles Lakers head coach Phil Jackson, who won a combined 11 NBA titles with the two franchises, was hired to become the President of the New York Knicks. He wanted to usher in a new era in New York. He wanted the team to run the Triangle to the same degree of success as he did when he was coaching the Bulls and Lakers. When he was asked who he wanted running the team as the head coach, the first name that came out of his mouth was Steve Kerr's.[vi]

It was an obvious choice. Steve Kerr knew the Triangle by heart after spending so much time playing under him back in the 90's. Phil knew how intelligent Steve Kerr was when he was still playing under him. He knew that he had absorbed everything he needed to learn from his mentor. This was despite the fact that Steve Kerr has never coached a game in his entire life.

The New York Knicks at that time were a puzzle. They had a top 10 player in Carmelo Anthony, who could even be the best offensive player on the planet whenever he is in the zone. But Anthony was one-dimensional. He could score with the best of them, but his game was limited to putting the ball in the basket. His defense was questionable, and he rarely played within the flow of the offense and opted to play isolation basketball more. The other pieces were not as attractive, either. The huge contracts of guys such as Tyson Chandler, Andre Bargnani, and Amar'e Stoudemire were clogging up the dockets and hindering financial flexibility. At that point of their respective careers, they were not even worth the money they were paid for. If anyone were to succeed to the position of Knicks head coach, he had to first deal with the personnel problem.

On the other hand, the Golden State Warriors were also offering Steve Kerr the same job with a more alluring package. Former head coach Mark Jackson had just stepped down after not seeing eye to eye with team ownership. He had already placed the pieces in the set for whoever would succeed to that position. Mark Jackson had turned a young Warriors team into playoff contenders particularly through their offensive firepower. Stephen Curry blossomed into a star while Klay Thompson was well on his way to becoming one. The complementary pieces such as Andre Iguodala and David Lee also were also more convincing for any coach to choose Oakland over the Big Apple. It was a young team that had the right pieces. The only thing that was needed was for the right guy to piece together the puzzle. Attracted by the Warriors' roster and wanting to stay closer to home in California, Steve Kerr would choose to go to Golden State instead of New York to pursue a new career as a head coach.

Despite the beauty that is the Golden State Warriors' roster makeup, nobody knew what to expect from rookie head coach Steve Kerr. They knew that the team was going to get to the playoffs one way or another whether it be through an easy route or past a rough road. But Steve Kerr shocked the world with the way he handled the roster and made them legitimate title contenders in a matter of months.

Before anyone realized it, the Golden State Warriors had become a show. On the offensive end, it all started with Steph Curry running pick-and-rolls or give-and-goes on the top of the key. Everybody was in constant motion looking for multiple screens to free themselves up when the pass came their way. All five guys on the floor were willing passers and were ready to shoot the ball if they were open. This gave a lot of flexibility for Steve Kerr on the offensive end. Everybody was moving to get shooters open. And by the time defenses realized what had happened, the ball was already through the hoop shot from beyond the three-point area by two of the greatest shooters the league has ever seen.

Steve Kerr would feast on both Curry's and Thompson's ability to hit jumpers from virtually everywhere on the floor. He kept the two shooters in constant motion while making sure his other role players were also moving and setting up picks. And if the Splash Brothers were not open, Kerr had other options in David Lee, Harrison Barnes, and Andre Iguodala.

But the offense did not revolve solely on either Curry or Thompson. The ball rotated so much on the offensive end that it was bound to find someone open as defenses were recovering and leaving their assignments unchecked. The Warriors' offense would become reminiscent of the one employed by Gregg Popovich against the Miami Heat during the 2014 NBA Finals. He called it "Summertime" because of how free the offense was. Pop made sure that players would only touch the ball for a maximum of half a second before they would pass it to another open player while defenders scrambled to recover. This kind of ball movement was an element that Steve Kerr got from his former mentor.

While Mark Jackson had already made the Warriors a fearsome offensive unit, the defensive job that Steve Kerr did in Golden State was what elevated the team to whole new heights. Kerr made use of Draymond Green's versatility on the defensive end. Green was big and strong enough to guard forwards and centers down at the low post. Out on the perimeter, he could keep up with guards, especially during switches on the pick and roll. Meanwhile, Steve Kerr paired him up with Andrew Bogut, who was always an intimidating defensive presence inside the paint because of his ability to block shots and bother layups. Then there was Andre Iguodala, who he had asked to come off the bench for the first time in his career. Iguodala had a reputation of being of the premier perimeter defenders because of his athleticism, strong body, and his anticipation.

Kerr's new offensive system and his ability to fully harness the defensive capabilities of his players resulted in the perfect marriage of offense and defense in an evolving league that demanded championship teams become elite on both ends of the floor. The good thing about all of it was that the Warriors were having a lot of fun on the floor. It was like Pop's Summertime, only that summer for the Warriors lasted for an entire season.

Steve Kerr would dominate the league in only his first season as a head coach. The Golden State Warriors would surprisingly win 67 games as opposed to only 15 losses. Kerr unleashed Stephen Curry, who was voted as the league's Most Valuable Player. Meanwhile, Klay Thompson became a valuable two-way player because of his offensive capabilities and his skills on the perimeter as a defender. Even

Draymond Green nearly became Defensive Player of the Year.

The Golden State Warriors marched into the playoffs as the heavy favorites to win the NBA title. But the competition was fierce. At one point, they were even trailing the Memphis Grizzlies, a classic slow-paced defensive team, in the second round of the playoffs. But the offense began clicking again, and the Warriors would dominate the rest of the playing field on their way to the 2015 NBA Finals.

A common belief in basketball is that jumpshooting teams never win titles. Such teams lived from the three-point line and would eventually die shooting from a distance without even having so much as a glimpse at the championship trophy. But Gregg Popovich, in 2014, proved that notion wrong by employing an offense that revolved around passing the ball so much to open up shooters on the perimeter. In 2015, Steve Kerr was well on his way to become the second coach to win an NBA title by relying on his team's jumpshooting ability.

The competition only got tougher in the Finals. The Cleveland Cavaliers were led by LeBron James, who was regarded as the best player on the planet and a man who was a veteran in the Finals. With James leading the way, the Cavs raced to a 2-1 series lead over the Golden State Warriors, who struggled to contain the best player on the planet.

Come Game 4, Steve Kerr made a decision that turned the tide for the Warriors. At the start of the season, he had found a way to convince Andre Iguodala that starting Harrison Barnes in place of him was for the betterment of the team and that it would be best if he would become the Warriors' designated Sixth Man. For the entire season, Iguodala bought into the idea after initially feeling bad about it. The wins made him feel better as he adjusted to his role as the Warriors' best bench player.

But in Game 4 of the NBA Finals, he was called by his coach to start for the team. But it was not in place of Harrison Barnes. Barnes was moved over to the power forward spot while starting power forward Draymond Green was upgraded to the center position. Center Andrew Bogut moved to the bench. At first, it was a risky move on the part of Steve Kerr. The Cavaliers had a large and bruising frontcourt of Timofey Mozgov and Tristan Thompson. If the Warriors could not handle them inside the paint on the defensive end, rebounding would also become a problem.

But the gamble worked for Kerr. The Golden State Warriors became an even more versatile defensive team with that small lineup. In pick and roll switches, Green and Barnes could keep up and cover the quick Cavalier guards, something that Bogut struggled to do. On the offensive end, all five players on the floor could shoot the ball. That took away the Cavs' ability to guard the paint because both big men had to step out to cover their man out on the perimeter. But, more importantly, it was Andre Iguodala's defensive work on LeBron James that ultimately led to the Warriors winning three straight games to clinch the NBA title.

For the first time since Pat Riley did it more than 30 years before in the 80's, Steve Kerr won the title as a rookie head coach. It was a rare feat for just about anyone in the history of the NBA. Phil Jackson could not do it even though he had Jordan and Pippen when he inherited the Bulls. He failed to do the same with Shaq and Kobe in Los Angeles. Gregg Popovich also could not do it though he had Tim Duncan and David Robinson manning the paint at the same time. But while Kerr was yet to reach the heights that his mentors were stepping on, he had become a champion far quicker than any other NBA coach before him had become. But being a champion was not foreign for Steve Kerr. After all, he had won five rings as a player under both Jackson and Pop.

Breaking Records

Just a few days into training camp while the Warriors were still high on the euphoria of an NBA title, Steve Kerr would announce that he was taking an indefinite leave of absence. He had been suffering from and headaches and pain due to back problems that were aggravated during the 2015 NBA Finals. Spinal fluid was leaking in his back, and he needed time to rehabilitate the injury before he could return to coaching the Warriors.

Luckily for Steve Kerr, the core remained the same. All the key players have already bought into the system that won them the 2015 NBA title. Moreover, they had already mastered all the sets and could run plays in their sleep. It also helped that the 2015 MVP Stephen Curry had taken his game to a whole new level during the offseason. Even other key pieces such as Klay Thompson and Draymond Green returned better than they were a year before. Though Steve Kerr was absent the entire 2015, his assistant Luke Walton acted as his mirror. At times, Walton looked and acted like Kerr on the sidelines. He would lead the Warriors to a record of 24-0 to start the season undefeated. It was only late in December when Golden State suffered their first loss. Under Walton, the Warriors were 39-4 and well on their way to breaking a record everybody thought was unbreakable.

While he was absent, Steve Kerr was still credited with the wins that his assistant Luke Walton was racking up for the Golden State Warriors. He would later call that rule "ridiculous." Nevertheless, Steve would return late in January 2016 to reprise his role as the head coach of the defending champions. By that time, the Warriors' confidence were at an all-time high, and Stephen Curry was well on his way to another MVP season.

In the final regular season game for the Golden State Warriors, the team had a record of 72-9. They were one win away from breaking the 1995-96 Chicago Bulls' record of 72 wins as against ten losses.

Interestingly enough, Steve Kerr was a part of that Bulls team that went 72-10 two decades earlier. But in easy fashion, Kerr and his Warriors would win their 73rd game of the season to surpass the record that was unbreakable for 20 years. Steve Kerr became the only man in league history to become a part of two 70-win teams. His first was when he was a player under Phil Jackson in Chicago, and the other one was when he was leading a historically great Golden State Warriors to 73 wins. With that unprecedented accomplishment, Steve Kerr was named the 2016 Coach of the Year.

But while Steve Kerr had broken records that season as a head coach, he would fail to repeat as a champion. In the 2016 NBA Finals, the team would face the Cleveland Cavaliers in a rematch of the previous year's championship series. The Warriors started out strong and would lead the series 3-1. But the Cavaliers adjusted accordingly to force Game 7 in Oakland, where the Cavs ultimately walked out as the NBA champions.

Coming into the 2016-17 season, Steve Kerr would add another weapon to his arsenal. If the Warriors were not already fearsome enough as they were, they were about to get even deadlier. Four-time scoring champion and 2014 NBA MVP Kevin Durant would join the mix as the Warriors had to sacrifice Harrison Barnes and Andrew Bogut to add a once-in-a-lifetime player into the roster. With KD at his disposal, Steve Kerr had a collection of four All-Stars, who made the Warriors the consensus favorites to win it all in the 2017 NBA Finals.

Kevin Durant would only make the Golden State Warriors more potent on offense. And though it was questionable whether Steve Kerr could make three great scorers in KD, Curry, and Thompson work together in the same offensive scheme, Steve Kerr's unselfish system of constant ball movement ensured that nobody in the team would selfishly dominate the shots and the possessions.

On March 28, 2017, in a win over the Houston Rockets, Steve Kerr became the fastest head coach in NBA history to reach 200 total wins not just in the NBA but any major professional sport in the United States. In only 238 total games, he achieved that marked and surpassed his former mentor Phil Jackson's record. Jackson earned his 200th regular season win after 270 games. In the MLB, it took Frank Chance 272 games to reach the 200-win mark. In the NFL, Don Shula did it in 282 games while Dan Bylsma did it in 316 games in the NHL.[viii] While he may be criticized for being able to win only because of his personnel, Steve Kerr has done more with what he had than arguably any coach in the history of the NBA.

And with Steve Kerr finishing the season with a 67-15 record, he became the first Warriors head coach to lead the team to three consecutive 50-win seasons. The Warriors also became the first team in nearly two decades to win 60 games three consecutive seasons. The last team to do it was the Chicago Bulls from 1996 to 1998. Steve Kerr was a member of the Bulls roster in those three seasons.

With the Golden State Warriors marching into the postseason with the best record in the league, and with an intact and healthy lineup, one can only imagine how much damage the team would do under Steve Kerr's offensive system. The Warriors are the favorites again to win the title and are in good form to win their second championship in a span of only three seasons. Steve Kerr, on the other hand, would be gunning for ring number seven.

Chapter 5: What Makes Steve Kerr a Good Leader

It Runs in the Blood

Steve Kerr has transformed the Golden State Warriors into the most dominant team in the league since the Lakers had the Shaq and Kobe tandem. He has been very successful as a leader, but to find out why, one would first have to look at Kerr's family history and the reason why he was in the NBA in the first place despite his athletic weaknesses.

Steve Kerr's leadership quality was a heritage of his family. He comes long from a long line of leaders, but in a different aspect of life. His grandfather Stanley Kerr was an academic and societal leader. Stanley lived his life as a professor of biochemistry before he decided to lead a group of volunteers that helped victims of the wars and strife in the Middle East. He eventually settled in Beirut, Lebanon to teach at the American University of Beirut.

Steve Kerr's father Malcolm was one of the leading figures in Middle Eastern studies. Having lived and studied in Beirut, he practically grew up knowing about the troubles of the Middle East. He would also follow Stanley's footsteps as an academic leader in the AUB before he relocated his family to California where he taught at UCLA. When Malcolm was named the president of the AUB, he would return to Beirut where he was eventually assassinated by religious extremists that resented American presence in Lebanon. Malcolm was one of the leading figures in helping usher a peaceful era in the Middle East.

While Steve Kerr's life was more peaceful than his grandfather and his father, he did, in fact, inherit leadership qualities from his predecessors. Steve Kerr grew up as a leader on his high school basketball team. He led not through his skills or his actions on the hard court, but by how he treated his teammates and friends alike. With his family away in Beirut, Steve Kerr treated his basketball teammates like his second family. He respected everyone and treated all of his teammates equally whether they were a part of the starting five or at the end of the bench.

Kerr's father has spent years being a mediator between different leaders from the Middle East. He was, in a sense, an academic diplomat. That was a leadership trait that Steve Kerr would inherit. He understood the importance of communicating with both sides. He understood what being understood was all about. Kerr would become a diplomat on the NBA hardcourt. He would listen to his players and get their sides while also communicating his ideas on how to make the team better. The son of an academic diplomat would turn into a kind of diplomat albeit in a different war.

Humor

More than his upbringing and genetics, Steve Kerr's personality was what brought people together under his leadership. In college, he was described as a player that everyone loved. The crowd may have loved him for his ability to hit the jump shot with so much precision, but in the locker room, players loved him for the way he treated everyone and how he genuinely cared. He would try to bring the best out of his teammates not in a demanding way, but by inspiring them to do better. His sense of humor also got the locker room lit up in laughter.

Steve Kerr would take the same kind of personality with him when he got to the NBA. When he was with the Suns, the Cavs, and the Magic, Kerr did have the opportunity to lead his teammates because of his youth and the presence of other veterans. It was not until he signed with the Chicago Bulls when Steve Kerr's great personality surfaced in the NBA.

While the Chicago Bulls were led by a trio of All-Stars at the prime of their careers, Steve Kerr was the one that got the locker room glued because of his personality. Michael Jordan might have been the one leading the scoring punch. Scottie Pippen might have been the one defending the best player on the court while being the primary playmaker on offense. Dennis Rodman might have been the one collecting 50% of all the misses. But it was Kerr who cracked jokes and absorbed all of Phil Jackson's teachings.

One of the most memorable jokes that Steve Kerr cracked when he was with the Bulls was during the 1997 victory rally. It was after winning the NBA title when Michael Jordan passed off from a double team to hit Steve Kerr open 17 feet away from the basket to make a wide open jumper that won the game. The man that hit the game winner for the championship team jokingly said that he had to take that shot because both MJ and Pippen wanted him to bail them out of a tough situation like he always did. It was a joke that got the Chicago crowd and the entire Bulls roster laughing.[ix]

Several years later when Michael Jordan returned to play for the Washington Wizards and when Steve Kerr was with the San Antonio Spurs, the two former teammates would match up on the perimeter. Kerr was telling his teammates to get him the ball on the post by shouting "Mouse in the house," a common phrase used by players whenever they had the size advantage against their defender.[ix]

Fast forward to February 2015 when Steve Kerr was chosen to become the head coach of the Western All-Stars, he would pull off another one of his classic jokes. He pulled his players together in a huddle and told them that he had a brilliant strategy to implement. The plan, in his words, involved one guy passing the ball to another guy, who passes the ball to another one until one of the players gets open for a shot. Though the purpose was to joke around, that was the essence of the Warriors' offense. They would pass the ball around so much that one would eventually find himself open. Of course, they had fun doing it to the tune of their coach's sense of humor.

After playing for the Bulls, Steve Kerr would later play the majority of the rest of his career under Gregg Popovich of the San Antonio Spurs. Gregg Popovich himself was always fond of joking around, albeit in a more serious approach. One of the many things he looked for when scouting players to sign was personality and a sense of humor. Steve Kerr was never one that lacked either of those.

Gregg Popovich himself said that Steve Kerr was a man that loved life more than anything else. Everybody on the team got along great with him. Kerr was always someone who was comfortable being himself and would laugh about his weaknesses and shortcomings. One of the many points of his humor was when he deprecates himself. He was always so comfortable and open about his being and personality that he often makes it the butt of his jokes. He laughs at himself, and his teammates and friends laugh along with him.[x]

As famous author George R.R. Martin wrote in *A Game of Thrones*,

"Never forget what you are, for surely the world will not. Make it your strength. Then it can never be your weakness. Armor yourself in it, and it will never be used to hurt you."

Unknowingly, Steve Kerr has lived his life following that mantra. Kerr knows his weaknesses and shortcomings but would rather joke about it than feel sorry for them. It was the kind of personality that Gregg Popovich would say that made him an attractive person to be around.[x]

Now, when you look at the Golden State Warriors' roster, it would seem that Steve Kerr's personality has rubbed off on his best key players. When talking about the Warriors' best player, one cannot fail to look the way of Stephen Curry. Aside from a lot of similarities in their names, Kerr and Curry have a lot of things in common, though the coach was never as accomplished of a player as his two-time MVP is.

Humility

Steve Kerr's personality also revolves around his humility. That was where his self-deprecating humor stemmed from. He was so humble about himself that he could joke about it. He would even often say that he was only lucky to be with the Warriors when the team already had all the pieces needed to win a title. But in that humility, there was always a fiery sense of competition burning. Kerr always got his players working hard and would teach them the value of balancing their life as a player and family man.[xi] He gets the best out of his players by asking them to work extra hard without sounding demanding.

Stephen Curry has shown to be the exact extension of that personality. While Curry may look arrogant on the court because of how much fun he has whenever he breaks ankles and hits three-pointers over the outstretched arms of his defenders, he conducts himself in the most humble way outside of the floor. Curry downplays the amount of work he puts into his game, yet videos of his everyday routine would show otherwise how much he trains to improve himself. He also always downplays his accomplishments and would instead point to his religious beliefs as the main reason for the amount of success he has seen in his career. Aside from all that, he has always found a balance between his maniacal work ethic and responsibility as a husband and father.

In everything he did as a player up until the time he coached the Warriors, Steve Kerr never put himself first. He always downplayed his accomplishments and put his ego at the bottom of his list of priorities. He always passes the credit to someone else. He credited how Mark Jackson put together the Warriors team before Kerr coached it. And when he gets asked about his journey, he always credits his former head coaches for everything he has learned. Kerr even once told his players that they could win the title without him and that this was their pursuit. He had already won his titles back when he was a player. It was only his job to guide the Warriors to a championship, but it was always within his players to be able to do it.

In Game 4 of the 2015 NBA Finals, the Warriors were down 1-2 in the series to the Cleveland Cavaliers. The famous move that made Kerr look like a genius was inserting Andre Iguodala into the starting lineup and benching Andrew Bogut in the process. Steve Kerr was lauded by the media and coaches for the brilliant move that made the team more responsive on defense and more dangerous on offense.

However, Steve Kerr would go on to tell the media that it was not his idea. The idea of putting Iguodala into the starting lineup came from Nick U'Ren, a young special assistant of the scouting staff. U'Ren himself texted assistant coach Luke Walton about the idea. Walton relayed it to Kerr, who had a discussion with his associates about the plan.[xii] The rest is history.

Kerr would credit U'Ren for that idea. However, Luke Walton would say that Steve Kerr was so humble in doing such an action. Walton would also say that, though it was not Kerr's idea, it was his decision that mattered. It was Kerr who ultimately decided to go with the notion of starting Iguodala though he did, in fact, admit and credited such a plan to one of the team's assistants.

The entire makeup of Steve Kerr's coaching staff shows how humble he is as a person knowing for a fact that he could not do the job alone and that he needed help from people who knew more than he did. His initial coaching staff included former head coach Alvin Gentry, who worked under him for the Phoenix Suns back in 2008-2010. It also included Ron Adams, one of the former defensive strategists when Kerr was with the Bulls. Kerr would even include young blood in Luke Walton and Jarron Collins to his coaching staff, believing that their minds would have fresh input in an ever-evolving league.[xii]

All of his assistants have nothing but praise for his humility. Adams said that Kerr is one of the most humble men he has ever worked with in his vast experience as a coach. Gentry would say that Steve Kerr was so humble and secure in his skin that he went out to hire people he knew could help him because he knew for himself that he did not have all the answers.[xii]

As an ultimate sign of his humility, Steve Kerr convinced the Warriors' ownership to lessen his salary when he was first approached to become the head coach under the belief that he was not deserving of a pay near what the veteran and accomplished coaches were receiving. The Warriors, of course, lessened their offer to the rookie head coach.[ix] Indeed, humility went a long way for Steve Kerr.

Communication

Gregg Popovich was often credited for his success with the San Antonio Spurs because of the way he openly communicates with his players and what he wants out of them. He once acted as the intermediary between Chris Webber and former Warriors head coach Don Nelson back in the 90's when he was an assistant at Golden State. He then made it a point that he would tell what his heart wanted to say whenever he talked to his players. He scolded everyone no matter how many All-Star appearances that player has made. At the same time, he also gave praise to the players at the end of his bench whenever they needed to be praised. That was one of the key takeaways that Steve Kerr got from the five-time champion coach.

Steve Kerr would promote the benefits of open communication the moment he became the new head coach of the Golden State Warriors. Like Pop, Kerr liked having communication with his players. He said his mind and always made it a point that whatever decision he made was for the betterment of the team and not of one single player.

One of the more famous moves that Steve Kerr did in his first season as a head coach was to move former All-Star wingman Andre Iguodala from the starting spot to the bench. Iguodala was always a starter since he entered the league. He was not accustomed to playing off the bench. But Kerr made the decision to accommodate rising forward, Harrison Barnes.

In his first two seasons since entering the league under Mark Jackson, Harrison Barnes was not happy playing off the bench. Of course, he had no reason to complain. Andre Iguodala was an established player who had made the All-Star team at one point in his career. Meanwhile, Barnes was still a new player that was growing and learning. Nevertheless, he was unhappy.

Steve Kerr would fly all the way to Barnes' home in Miami during the offseason to talk to his young forward. Nobody knows exactly what happened during the meeting. But when Harrison Barnes was asked, all he had to say was that he asked Steve Kerr a lot of difficult questions he could think of. According to Barnes, Kerr answered all of them with utmost honesty. No sugar-coating and no sweet talk. That was what made Barnes happy.[iv]

Barnes was shocked with what his coach did. Some coaches would fly to their star players' homes and would be content with just texting or calling the other guys. But Barnes was happy with how Kerr was committed to going through certain lengths just to be able to communicate with everyone on the team. That act alone sent a message of how dedicated of a leader the new head coach was.

While accommodating Harrison Barnes as a starter was the easier part, the tricky part was asking a former All-Star to come off the bench. Steve Kerr would personally ask Andre Iguodala to play a reserve role and lead the second unit. It was a tough thing to ask from a veteran that had achieved so much as a starter. He was an All-Star and was once an integral part of the Team USA in their gold medal victories. But Iguodala acceded to his coach's request.[ix]

What Steve Kerr made Iguodala understand was that the team needed him to lead the bench and that they needed Harrison Barnes to flourish at the starting spot. Barnes had struggled all year before Kerr took over. With the starting spot, he could get better looks and less defensive pressure because of all the attention that Curry and Thompson would be getting from the opposing defense. Indeed, Barnes would flourish and become better as a starter.[ix]

Meanwhile, Steve Kerr would praise Iguodala for such a huge sacrifice. Andre Iguodala was not initially happy about the decision, but realized that it was for the betterment of the team when they were winning in bunches. Kerr loved the idea of Iguodala leading the bench because of his ability to do everything at a high level. He was the one stabilizing what would have otherwise been a chaotic second unit. By accepting the role, Iguodala also sent a huge message to the locker room. He was an All-Star and gold medallist, yet he took a step back to let his younger teammates grow.[xii] That was what a leader would do. That was what Steve Kerr had instilled in Iguodala.

And while he initially did not plan to do it, Steve Kerr would also have another former All-Star accept a lesser role from the bench. David Lee had become an All-Star both as a Knick and Warrior. However, a bevy of injuries had kept Lee out of the lineup for stretches of the season. His first injury early on was a stepping stone for Draymond Green to show his defensive versatility and his ability to be an all-around power forward. Green would earn praise and would see himself becoming the full-time starter at the power forward spot.

When Lee came back from injury, he became an afterthought. He hardly played, and if Kerr would even play him, he did so sparingly. This led to people thinking that Lee might hate Kerr for rarely playing him. But Lee himself would always say that he and Steve Kerr had a strong relationship. And if one would see how David Lee reacts from the bench, he does it so happily. He was still his old self, cracking jokes and smiling whenever his teammates made good plays. Steve Kerr kept him happy.[xiii]

But it was David Lee's change from a mental standpoint that kept him happy while rarely even seeing minutes under Steve Kerr. Kerr always preached the importance of sacrifice and team play. Lee understood. Out of all the players that had flourished under Mark Jackson, it was David Lee who had to sacrifice most. He was an All-Star under Jackson, but played sparingly under Kerr without complaining about it because he knew how his sacrifice would put together what eventually became a championship.[xiii]

On his part, Lee had already proven himself as a double-double monster and as an All-Star. He knew that people knew what he was capable of. What was more important to him at that point was to figure out how to contribute to the title run.[xiii] Now with the San Antonio Spurs, David Lee approaches the game in the same unselfish way he did when he was with the Golden State Warriors.

But it was not only with Barnes, Iguodala, and Lee that Steve Kerr had talks with. He would go as far as to personally speak with his players regarding his plans with the roster and how he believed he could take them to the next level if they would go along with what he had in mind. Kerr would even go as far as Australia to meet with big man Andrew Bogut, who resided there during the offseason. The lengths that Kerr had to take to communicate with his players were incredible but nothing short of what was needed for a championship team.

Luck

While nobody would ever credit luck as one of Steve Kerr's leadership secrets, it has nevertheless played a significant part in his success. Kerr himself would even say that he was always lucky. He was lucky to have inherited a core of players that only needed a push to succeed. He would say he was fortunate to have had a coaching staff with enough experience and knowledge of the game. And he would say that he was lucky to have been under the wings of some of the greatest coaches in the history of the league.

However, Steve Kerr has always been modest about his success. Whether he was lucky or not, Kerr had a better hand than luck in driving the Warriors to a championship run in only his rookie season. But there is one aspect of that dominant title run that one would give credit to Lady Luck's hand at helping Steve Kerr put the pieces together.

Back when Mark Jackson was still the head coach of the Golden State Warriors, his offense primarily revolved around Steph Curry out on the perimeter and David Lee inside the paint. Since getting drafted by the New York Knicks several seasons back, Lee was always known for his knack of knowing where the rebound was going to fall. He used his instinct and wide frame to position himself for rebounds and putback opportunities. Inside the paint, Lee was an unstoppable finisher that could average 20 points and ten rebounds in any given season. He was an All-Star that Mark Jackson used to his advantage.

But in Jackson's final year with the Warriors, several members of his coaching staff had given him the idea of benching Lee in favor of Draymond Green. As good of a rebounder, finisher, and passer that Lee was, he could not defend. He was a defensive liability that could not stretch the floor on the offensive end. Defense was the biggest problem for the Warriors during Jackson's run as the head coach. And while Lee was a liability on that end, Draymond Green was quietly making himself known as a versatile defender that could lock up big men and perimeter players alike. But Mark Jackson dismissed the idea of starting Green in place of Lee because the latter was too good of an offensive weapon to bench.[xiv]

When Steve Kerr was about to take the coaching reigns, he had the idea of implementing changes that Mark Jackson was not willing to. Instead of putting the ball too much in Curry's hands, he wanted it to move. Instead of starting Andre Iguodala, he wanted to bench him in favor of Barnes. However, starting Green over Lee was not one of the ideas he had in mind. He was still in favor of making David Lee one of the key players in that starting lineup.

It was in November when David Lee hurt his left hamstring and was sidelined for weeks. While it was unlucky on the part of Lee that he had been injured, Steve Kerr was fortunate. Kerr had previously intended to keep starting Lee if he stayed healthy, but the two-time All-Star got hurt. For Kerr, he was lucky he had Draymond Green. Green would transform into the league's most versatile and unique defensive force because of his ability to cover the pick and roll and of his toughness in handling opposing post players. Best of all, his furious mindset and fighting spirit made him the Warriors' emotional leader.

Aside from David Lee's injury and Draymond Green's eventual emergence, Steve Kerr also had luck playing for him when both Kevin Love and Kyrie Irving of the Cleveland Cavaliers were hurt during the 2015 NBA Finals. While Kerr would have still had the advantage had the Cavs been healthy, the absence of the two All-Stars only made it easier for him to secure his first title as a coach and his sixth overall in the NBA. Nevertheless, as what is popularly said, luck is a residue of design. Had it not been for Kerr's preparations, luck would not have come by his way as a leader.

Being Dynamic

One of the reasons why both Phil Jackson and Gregg Popovich were so successful as head coaches was their dynamic approach to the game of basketball. On Phil's part, he had a system that he never touched. He always stuck to the Triangle Offense, but he was dynamic in the way he handled his personnel. Remember, he had an alpha male in Michael Jordan, whose competitive nature he had to get in check, while also trying to control the instability of a guy like Dennis Rodman. And in Los Angeles, Phil Jackson had to be dynamic in trying to handle two of the biggest egos in basketball—Shaquille O'Neal and Kobe Bryant.

For Gregg Popovich, the Spurs head coach was always known for his ability to adjust on the fly. He chose players that had certain character traits and personalities that he liked. His dynamic side comes out whenever he changes his evolving system according to the personnel he has. When he had David Robinson and Tim Duncan, he played a slow-paced style that adjusted to his big men. And when he later passed the offense down to Tony Parker, he had the Spurs playing faster than ever and shooting three-pointers in bunches.

That dynamic trait was one of the things that Steve Kerr picked up in his years playing under those two great head coaches. At Golden State, Steve Kerr learned to become dynamic by understanding the natures of every player he had on the roster and adjusted to them accordingly. During practices, he often stressed the importance of selflessness. He had to convince players in different ways to let them know how important it was to think of the team first before the individual. He learned how to let his players buy into his philosophy of sacrifice and hard work.

Kerr himself would say that both Jackson and Pop were dynamic coaches that were able to help their team buy into their beliefs by stressing their principles, being intelligent, having a sense of humor, and possessing enough charisma. In a sense, Steve Kerr became a dynamic leader by knowing how to pick up the best traits of two coaches that could not be any more different in the way they approached the game.[xv]

Experience

His genetic ability to lead and his personality may be the best reasons why Steve Kerr is as good of a leader as he is right now, but the championship coach credits his life experience as to why he is so successful as a leader. By experience, Kerr meant his ride as a player under successful coaches such as Lenny Wilkens when he was with the Cavs, Phil Jackson when he was playing for the Bulls, and Gregg Popovich when he was winning in San Antonio.

Time and time again, Steve Kerr stresses the fact that his knowledge as an NBA coach and his leadership qualities were some of the things he only picked up from the coaches he had the pleasure working with when he was still playing. He claims to look at his mentors' best qualities and take them to heart in his journey as a leader and coach.

Take Phil Jackson, for instance. Jackson is popularly known as the Zen Master in the NBA for his spiritual approach to the game of basketball. Because of his practice of Zen, Jackson stayed calm and collected, even during the most difficult times of a match. He never gets flustered or stressed. Even when the opposing team is on a good run, he does not call a timeout and would lets his players solve the puzzle themselves. You rarely see the easy-going head coach yelling and screaming at the sidelines because of dumb plays or bad calls. He handled the egos of the superstars he had coached with when he was Chicago and later in Los Angeles. Jackson knew how to let his stars buy into the team aspect of basketball while also allowing them to flourish their way.

On the other hand, Gregg Popovich approaches coaching in a different way. Because of his military background, Pop is a stern and stoic disciplinarian that is never afraid to get in the face of his players whenever they sway from the game plan or his instructions. He makes his emotions known to referees and players but always makes sure he does not let his anger get the best of him. Pop would stress the importance of discipline and communication and would even go as far as yelling at his best players to get his point across. Even when he shows his soft and caring side, Gregg Popovich still seems like a strict disciplinarian that only seeks to get the best out of his players and staff.

In his experience working with those coaches, who both combine for 16 NBA championships to date, Steve Kerr stays true to his character while also incorporating qualities he deemed best would help his team succeed. Like Jackson, Kerr remains calm and collected. He rarely gets frustrated on the sidelines and allows his players free range in solving problems on the floor. Meanwhile, he also stresses the value of discipline and communication. He gets his point across by communicating with each player on his roster while also letting them know that discipline during practices is one of the keys to hard work.

Best of all, Steve Kerr learned from both coaches that having a good sense of humor during practices and games allows the team to lighten up and have fun while striking daggers into the hearts of their opponents. It was his experience working under some of the greatest coaches in league history was what helped him improve as a leader and as a coach by seeing all the qualities that players would like to have in their coaches.

But, make no mistake, Steve Kerr was always a man comfortable in his skin. He stayed true to his personality and would never try to shy away from his character. As Gregg Popovich would put it, it is Kerr's personality that attracts people to his side and makes him a good leader. Even as a player, Kerr also showed qualities as a leader and as a coach considering that both Jackson and Popovich saw the makings of one in him. While experience made Steve Kerr into a better leader that he is, it was that same experience under great coaches that ultimately made him realize that coaching was always his calling as a person.

Chapter 6: How Steve Kerr Maximizes Player Potential

One of the main reasons as to why Steve Kerr's Golden State Warriors have been so dominant and successful does not stem from how well his stars are playing. Everyone on the team seems to contribute to the larger cause, much like how Gregg Popovich taps into his role players' hidden talents and uses them effectively to complement his key guys.

The ball movement that Steve Kerr stresses to his team has given life to the otherwise dead careers of some of the Golden State Warriors' key bench players. Shaun Livingston was once seen as a future star in the league before his gruesome knee injury. Since then, he has bounced from team to team and never saw much success until he became the backup point guard to Steph Curry at Golden State. Livingston started shooting better from the field since joining the Warriors precisely because of the ball movement, which found him in his open spots. Kerr would often call his number first whenever the starters were stagnant. He scored 16 points in the first half alone in Game 1 of the Western Conference Finals against the Rockets in 2015.

Meanwhile, another backup guard who once played for the Warriors in Kerr's first two years, Leandro Barbosa, provided a lot of spark off the bench, though many believed his best years were already done after he left Phoenix back when his now head coach was still an executive with the Suns. Though he was not as quick as he used to be, Barbosa still provided excelled playing under the fast-paced offense of the Warriors. Barbosa scored 11 points in Game 1 of the 2016 NBA Finals against the Cleveland Cavaliers. He, Livingston, and Iguodala combined for 43 points off the bench in a match where none of the Warriors' starters were doing well.

Guard Ian Clark, who barely played on any of his previous teams before coming over to Golden State, has also become a spark off the bench for the Warriors precisely because of his ability to hit the open jumper. He has played his best years as a Warrior because of how much Steve Kerr trusts in his jumpshot.

Though he would only play 16 minutes per game under Steve Kerr compared to when he was averaging nearly 20 minutes a night with his previous teams, center Marreese Speights has averaged his best scoring numbers during the 2014-15 season in Kerr's first season as a head coach. Though his minutes would dwindle later on, his ability to hit the jumper from the perimeter for a big man was a premium for Steve Kerr's system.

It was a surprise for many that Kerr was able to use Mo Speights so effectively. The Warriors brought him in during Jackson's final year because of his jumper, but that was all he could do. He shot the ball the moment he thought he had a good shot at making the basket. He even showed up out of shape a season before. In a sense, he was not the ideal player under Kerr's system. However, Kerr trusted him enough to run a play for him where he would get an easy elbow jumper. But Steve Kerr, as he does, often dismisses the credit he gets. He claims to have only told Speights to come into the season in shape, and that everything else was the big man's doing.[xiv]

Even wingman Brandon Rush, whose career nearly went down the drain after injuries cost him in his first run as a Warrior, was impressive under Steve Kerr especially when he was filling up as a starter in place of Harrison Barnes, who was injured for a good part of the 2015-16 season. Rush hit the three-pointer with precision and would defend the perimeter nearly as well as Barnes did.

Looking at some of the role players that have come and go for the Warriors during Steve Kerr's three seasons with the team, one can only guess how Kerr was so successful in getting the best out of them. He allowed them to play their specialties and off the skills and abilities of the core stars of the team. Shooters like Barbosa, Clark, and Rush were able to get themselves open because of the defensive attention that the stars were getting. At 6'7", Livingston found matchup problems because bigger and longer defenders were more focused on Curry and Thompson out on the perimeter. Even the backup big men thrived in the paint because of how much defensive attention the shooters were getting.

It also all boils down to how much trust Steve Kerr gives his role players. Though Kerr relies a lot on the heavy lifting of his stars and starters, the main guys barely play over 34 minutes per game. Kerr usually limits his starters' minutes to about 33 a night, not only because the Warriors were beating opponents before the fourth quarter even starts, but because of how much he trusts his bench to keep the ship afloat when the starters are resting. The level of confidence he puts into his role players allows them to thrive and run the system as if they were the starters in the first place. It was a lesson he picked up from Gregg Popovich, who always made sure that the team maintained the same level of intensity on both ends of the floor even though the starters were on the bench resting.

Although Steve Kerr has learned to rely on maximizing his bench players' potential, everything still starts and ends with his star players, Stephen Curry, Klay Thompson, Draymond Green, and Kevin Durant. Mark Jackson may have already laid down the foundations, particularly on Curry and Thompson, but it was Kerr who unleashed those players' full potential.

Stephen Curry has been the longest tenured member of the Golden State Warriors. He has been with the team since 2009 when Don Nelson was still running the show. Knee injuries slowed him down early on, but Curry learned to adapt to his injuries and compensated elsewhere. He would grow into a crowd favorite and terrific offensive player when Mark Jackson took over as the head coach when new owner Joe Lacob took over the team.

Under an all-time great point guard such as Mark Jackson, Curry thrived under the pick and roll. He had the ball in his hands so much that the rest of the players' job was to allow him to free himself up from his defenders. They would set endless screens for him out on the perimeter to make sure he was wide open. Steph Curry would blossom into a star under Mark Jackson.

Jackson did nearly the same to Klay Thompson. Mark Jackson was blessed to have played with an all-time great shooter such as Reggie Miller back in the 90's. Miller's job was simple. He was running off screens to get to an open spot and shot the ball whenever it found him. Jackson was often the one feeding Miller the ball for wide open perimeter jumpers. Thompson played a similar role for the Warriors as a secondary shooter behind Curry.

However, the problem with the Warriors under Mark Jackson was that they played the isolation and pick-and-roll too much. It looked similar to the 90's era of basketball where Jackson thrived as a passer, but it was a system that could not fully reap the benefits of the Warriors' makeup. For a team that had a lot of good shooters and passers, the Warriors were dead last in passes per possession back in the 2013-14 season in Jacksons' final year with the team. Simply put, they did not pass the ball often enough to find open shooters.[xiv] They were content with getting their best players free from their defenders to give them wide open shots. If not that, they allowed Curry to play isolation ball and kill his defender off the dribble.

Under Steve Kerr, both Curry and Thompson would play fewer minutes than they did under Jackson. However, they would score more points and become more efficient in whatever time they saw on the floor playing under Kerr. Curry remained the central star on the offensive end. The team would still often set screens up for him or to give him an open lane out on the perimeter. But the amount of ball movement in the team allowed Steph Curry to pick his spots and shoot jumpers he was comfortable with. He would win the MVP in 2015, but would reach his full potential in 2016 when he led the league in scoring and became the first ever unanimous MVP in NBA history.

While Curry's ascension to the top of the NBA was largely a product of the Warriors' system, the amount of trust that Steve Kerr puts on his best player has gotten the two-time MVP's confidence at an all-time high. As Luke Walton would put it, Kerr gave Curry full freedom in running the offense and looking for his shot. Never the selfish player, Steph Curry would use the freedom to run plays he saw fit, but would also pick his spots whenever he felt hot. There is no wonder why Curry would just suddenly jack up shots from 30 feet away from the basket while Kerr did not even mind at all from the bench.

In a way, Kerr and Curry have developed a symbiotic relationship where one feeds off the other. Steve Kerr was always known for his quiet competitive spirit. He and Stephen Curry would get into free throw shooting duels after practices. While Kerr is a legendarily accurate free throw shooter, Curry has developed into a better one. The results would almost always tilt in the way of the two-time MVP. Rather than sulking or hiding the fact that he often loses to his player, Kerr would publicize how much Curry owns him in their friendly competitions. This has allowed Curry to put a lot of trust on Kerr as well.[xvi]

Luke Walton would tell you that Steve Kerr allows Curry and the entire Warriors team to improvise on their own. It was a kind of freedom where the coaches allow their players to think for themselves and not be slaves to their playbook.[xvi] They read the defense on their own and attack accordingly. That was why Curry led the league in scoring during the 2015-16 season. That was also why Klay Thompson was allowed all the leeway to shoot whenever he had one of his legendary hot streaks.

Speaking of Thompson, the man regarded as the second-best shooter in the league suddenly turns into the best shooter the world has ever seen whenever he is on a hot streak. Not even Curry can match Klay's output whenever he felt like everything he was putting up was going in. The team would always find a way to get Thompson open whenever he was shooting hot from the perimeter. The reason as to why they do so is because of the trust that Kerr puts into his players. Kerr believed that Thompson would get his shots whenever his confidence was at an all-time high. When he is on a hot streak, there are no plays called. The Warriors only set screens to open Klay Thompson up and trust that he makes his shots. And 99% of the time, he does so.

The philosophy as to why Steve Kerr puts so much trust into giving his main players so much freedom to make plays and adjust accordingly to the defensive schemes they were seeing is that he believes that defenses would also change whenever they saw how much freedom to shoot Curry and Thompson had on the floor. It does not matter when Curry misses his 30-foot jumpers or when Thompson fails to hit six consecutive shots. The defense would always adjust knowing that Steve Kerr trusts that his players can make those kinds of shots.[xvi] And if they did not adjust accordingly, they would eventually see Steph Curry hitting shots from near the half court line or Klay Thompson suddenly making ten straight jumpers in a row.

Even Kevin Durant has seen the benefits of such a free-flowing and unselfish offense. Since joining the league in 2007, Kevin Durant has been one of the best scorers in the NBA. He would win the scoring title four times in his career as the primary offensive weapon of the Oklahoma City Thunder. But during his tenure with the Thunder, the team often played isolation ball and would rely on him and point guard Russell Westbrook to make plays for themselves. Like the pre-Kerr Warriors, the Thunder were always one of the teams that lacked ball movement and passes per possession.

After years of playing over 36 minutes per game, KD would join the Warriors and play under 34 minutes a night for Steve Kerr. However, despite seeing fewer minutes and possessions, Durant has been the beneficiary of the Warriors' ball movement and freedom on offense, which allowed him to free himself up for open scoring opportunities more than he ever did for the Thunder. Kevin Durant would have the lowest scoring average he has seen since his second year in the league, but his field goal shooting percentage and shooting efficiency has been at an all-time high precisely because of the trust Kerr puts on him and the other players on the offensive end.

While the freedom and confidence that Kerr gives his team are huge reasons as to why his players have been successful on the offensive end, the biggest reason for their success on defense was the trust and opportunity that the rookie champion coach gave Draymond Green. Green was not supposed to become a Defensive Player of the Year contender. He was not expected to be an All-Star. He was expected to be content with playing a backup role to David Lee at the power forward position. But Lee got injured early in 2014. That was when Kerr unleashed what would soon become the most versatile and unique defensive force in the NBA.

At barely 6'7", Draymond Green is undersized for the power forward position. He may even be shorter than other small forwards. He was always aware of the fact that he was too short for his playing position. Throughout his life, he always knew he lacked in one aspect or another. He was often mocked for his lack of leaping ability. He stayed chubby and overweight for most of his basketball career. And he was always described as a tweener between the small forward and the power forward positions—too unathletic to be a small forward and too small to be a power forward.[xiv]

When he was called up to start in place of the injured Lee, one of Draymond Green's first games as a starter was against the Denver Nuggets. Defending the 6'8" Kenneth Faried, all that Green could hear from the Nuggets' bench was the phrase "He's too little." They were asking Faried to take advantage of what was perceived to be a mismatch against the smaller Green.

But little did they know that Draymond Green worked on his conditioning and shape just shortly after Steve Kerr took over in 2014. He lost weight and transformed his body. Green became quicker and more athletic while maintaining the same strength and defensive balance he was always known for when he was drafted.

With Steve Kerr trusting Green to anchor the defensive end of the floor, the man that was described as "too little" has become the only player in the league that can guard Chris Paul out on the perimeter during switches. He can stop a streaking LeBron James on his track during transition, contain DeMarcus Cousins on the low post, and body up Dwight Howard during rebound opportunities.

What Green lacked in athleticism and size he made up for in his intensity and willingness to do everything just to win. In a sense, Steve Kerr had his Dennis Rodman in Draymond Green. While Green was not as flamboyant and unorthodox as Rodman, he remains just as fiery and fierce as The Worm was. In a locker room of soft-spoken and silent players, Draymond Green evolved into the Warriors' emotional leader aside from being the best defensive player as far as stats would show. Kerr allowed him to be himself and did not try to contain him.

Whenever Green had his emotional outbursts, Kerr allowed him to do so because he thought it was for the betterment of the team to know what was on the mind of one of their leaders. Green remembered how he once shouted at Steve Kerr from the court onto the sidelines because of a play. Kerr shouted back at him. In the next dead ball situation, Draymond Green apologized to Kerr for shouting. Instead of saying Green was wrong, Kerr further empowered his fiery forward by telling him he loves his passion and that he would not try in any way to stop him from being himself.[xvi] That was how Kerr maximized and unleashed his best defensive asset.

With those said, the one main reason as to how Steve Kerr was able to maximize his assets and his players' potential is that he trusts them so much. He trusted that his role players would be able to fill in the holes of the starters and to play off of the stars. He trusted his primary scorers Curry, Thompson, and Durant with so much freedom on the offensive end. Lastly, he also trusted Draymond Green to anchor the defensive end of the floor and in maintaining the fiery intensity that the Warriors have been lacking.

It is this level of trust and freedom that has allowed the Warriors to excel on their own. Not a lot of coaches are willing to put their faith into players he barely knew or to guys that are yet to prove themselves in the league. But Steve Kerr did it to a level that can only be rivaled by that of Popovich himself. He let his players grow and develop at their pace knowing and trusting that whatever they did was for the betterment of the entire Warriors team.

Chapter 7: What is Steve Kerr's System?

Steve Kerr himself would like to credit his entire experience playing under great coaches such as Lenny Wilkens, Phil Jackson, and Gregg Popovich. After being in television broadcast for eight years, Kerr had a lot of time to study defenses and plays from other coaches. He reportedly even spent two years studying and preparing to be a coach by writing plays, reading books, and watching film. And when he was an executive in Phoenix, he also learned a thing or two from then-head coach Mike D'Antoni. Those experiences are exactly the reason why Steve Kerr's system in the Golden State Warriors seems to be the culmination of the knowledge he gained as a player, broadcaster, and executive.

With the help of a good offensive coach like Alvin Gentry (now head coach of the New Orleans Pelicans), who was part of his original staff, Steve Kerr has developed an offensive system that combines everything he learned under his coaches and from his years studying plays and systems. Gentry would call this a "melting pot" because of how he and Kerr were able to combine several aspects of legendary coaches' systems into one offensive scheme that worked to perfection for the Warriors.[xiv]

What used to be a one-dimensional offense that always looked to free Steph Curry up through multiple screens and pick-and-roll actions turned into one that looked like a cross of sorts of familiar systems we have seen in the past. What seems like a rhythm and flow offense, Kerr uses remnants of the Triangle Offense through high-post-actions from the post passer like Bogut or Green. He also uses drag screens and sideline tilts similar to how Mike D'Antoni did when he was in Phoenix to free shooters up from the perimeter. And what was clear was that Kerr had utilized the motion and loop offense that Gregg Popovich used to perfection against the Miami Heat during the 2014 NBA Finals.[xiv]

In line with Pop's system, Warriors GM Bob Myers hired Kerr on the basis that he could bring the team the same kind of ball movement and flow that he saw from the Spurs during the 2014 Finals. Myers thought that the way the Spurs were moving the ball so well to make it hard for opposing defenses to recover was the right way to play the game of basketball. He liked what Steve Kerr presented to them and liked how Kerr stressed ball and people movement.

Regarding the motion and loop system, Kerr often utilizes the ability of his big men(Andrew Bogut and now Zaza Pachulia) to make passes and dribble hand-offs at the top of the key. This starts a motion and loop where shooters would curve and cut until all five players on the floor eventually get to touch the ball in their pursuit of finding the best shot possible. What often results is a wide-open shot from the three-point area or an easy high-percentage look deep in the paint.

While it may also sound odd at first, Steve Kerr credits a lot of the offensive success to Steph Curry, who averaged 30 points during the 2015-16 season, for allowing himself to play off the ball so much less than he had to under Mark Jackson. Under Jackson, Curry almost always had the ball to run pick and rolls and go through screens. However, under Kerr, Curry found himself running through screens and cutting to the basket without the ball in his hands. Even without the ball in his hands, Steph Curry has risen to the top of the NBA's scoring charts precisely because of his decreased possessions.

Steve Kerr's logic as to how Steph Curry managed to become a better scorer while also making the Warriors' offense better by lessening his possessions is simple. Kerr believes that by allowing Curry to run around the court to find openings and run off screens makes the defense adjust to him so much that other players get open. And when opposing defenses try to keep their eyes on the other players, Curry gets his looks easier. It was a read and react kind of play. And with the rest of the Warriors often stepping up, Steph Curry gets himself open more than he ever has in his career.[xvii]

While Steve Kerr's offense may look more like Gregg Popovich's Spurs, the champion coach would often look and act more like Phil Jackson on the sidelines. He smiles and takes games easy as if he did not have a single problem in the world much like how Phil did when he was coaching. Kerr is calm, relaxed, and rarely gets flustered. But what gets him flustered, aside from turnovers, is how he could not get all of his guys to play. Like Phil Jackson, Steve Kerr gives equal opportunities to everyone in the team. He allows even the last guy on the roster list to play a few minutes as a reward from a successful practice. This has not only allowed all the players to grow in confidence, but it also makes it more difficult for opposing teams to prepare their defense considering the number of guys they have to scout for.

But Steve Kerr's system was not initially at its peak form when he first made the Warriors run it during offseason tournaments. The problem that Kerr saw were turnovers because of all the ball movement they were doing. The Warriors were also running so many plays that it got them confused, which ultimately led to turnovers. What Steve Kerr did in response was cut the plays down. From over 20 plays, he had his team running five good ones that they needed to perfect.

How Steve Kerr made his players improve their plays was elementary. He had them doing fundamental drills only middle schoolers did. Andrew Bogut remembers how Kerr made them run basic passing drills at the start of training camp to their frustration. Over time, they came to accept the underlying rationale of the drills. Kerr was trying to get them to buy into selflessness. He already knew how good they were at making passes. He only needed them to buy into the actual instinct of making the right pass instead of looking to take difficult shots. With that, the Warriors bought into the culture of selflessness and team play that Steve Kerr envisioned before he started coaching the team.

While offense may be the Warriors' calling card, it was their improvement under Steve Kerr on the defensive end that truly allowed them to become arguably the best team in the history of basketball. For Steve Kerr, it all started with personnel and how they looked for players that were not necessarily already good on defense, but had the tools and potential to be great at that end of the floor.

Throughout his years as a coach of the Warriors, Kerr has had the pleasure of working with long and quick players that could defend the paint and cover the perimeter during switches. Guys like Andre Iguodala, Klay Thompson, Draymond Green, Harrison Barnes,

Shaun Livingston, and Kevin Durant are all capable of handling themselves because of their size, length, and defensive versatility.

In a sense, Steve Kerr and his staff have found a way to utilize their length whenever teams switch via the pick and roll, which is the most frequent play used in basketball today. He uses switches to his advantage by utilizing players that could cover both the perimeter and the paint well.[xviii] Simply put, there are no mismatches on defense whenever Steve Kerr puts on a lineup of long and quick guards and forwards.

While other teams such as the Memphis Grizzlies would use a slow pace to enforce their defense, Kerr makes use of the fast pace to his advantage by employing a lineup that can cover all grounds. His guards can guard from positions one to three on the court. His forwards can switch out on guards and even defend centers. Meanwhile, he has always made sure that his big man in the middle could stand his ground and guard the paint. Shot blocking centers such as Bogut, Pachulia, and even JaVale McGee have found a home in Golden State.

And with the NBA transitioning into a smaller fast-paced style of basketball, Kerr and his staff followed suit on the defensive end. Today, agile teams that love to shoot out on the perimeter would own defenses that rely on big men manning the middle. Had this been the 80's and 90's when pairs of seven footers were guarding the paint, it would have been an entirely different story. But now, slow seven footers are forced to move out on the perimeter to guard shooting big men or switch on to guards way outside the three-point line.

With the Warriors, there was no way any team can take advantage of slow big men that are forced to cover the perimeter because Kerr makes sure that everyone on the court can cover the perimeter and the paint. Draymond Green has become the anchor of this defense because of his versatility. He can switch out on the perimeter to cover point guards while also bodying up centers in the paint. He is the key to what is called the Warriors' "Lineup of Death," which utilizes Green at the center position while four other perimeter players back him up.

This Lineup of Death may be more of an offensive strategy considering the amount of perimeter looks that opposing teams may have to give up. However, it is also a defensive tactic because all five guys out on the court can cover multiple positions and are not prone to mismatch problems in today's evolving NBA where centers are shooting three-pointers and are not as big as the ones that roamed the paint 10 or 20 years ago.

Simply put, the Golden State Warriors under Steve Kerr have become a dominant team on both ends of the floor precisely because of their ability to move the ball so much on offense while also always moving on defense to cover multiple positions and to help out on switches. This kind of a system is what Kerr has always envisioned all along. It is five guys out on the floor being selfless on both ends of basketball to reach a common goal of winning the championship.

Chapter 8: Key Takeaways

A major takeaway to how Steve Kerr leads his team is through his personality. While people have different personalities, Kerr uses a combination of humility, humor, and openness in leading his players. Not everyone may be funny, but anyone can make people smile in their way, even if it is not exactly how Steve Kerr would do it. And humility is a trait anyone can have for as long as he is comfortable in his skin, much like Kerr is. Best of all, in a team game, open communication has always made the difference. Nobody can ever discount how much communication can change a relationship and the team's dynamics.

As far as maximizing his players' skills are concerned, the main takeaway that one can get from Steve Kerr's story is the level of trust he puts into his players. These guys are in the NBA for a reason. They have reached a level of skill and mastery of fundamentals that no other group of players in the world have reached. Kerr knows that for a fact, and he trusts in the abilities of all 12 players out on the floor.

Kerr trusts his players so much that he allows his bench to take over games whenever starters are stagnant or not in rhythm. Nobody could ever forget how the Warriors' bench controlled Game 1 of the 2016 NBA Finals against the Cleveland Cavaliers. It is a level of trust unseen from any other coach in the world save for Gregg Popovich, who served as one of Kerr's mentors.

The level of confidence Kerr gives his star players also allows the guys on the court to move and perform with a sense of freedom knowing that whatever they do out there, they have their coach's back. While the system may be the reason for the flow and rhythm we see from the Warriors, the freedom that Steve Kerr gives them also allows them to play with so much fun and fluidity. Turnovers may come and go from time to time, but Kerr trusts that his guys would always make the right decisions instead of just policing and disciplining them for every wrong action they might do.

Steve Kerr's trust in his team transcends roles for both coaches and players alike. His famous Lineup of Death that he employed against the Cavs during the 2015 NBA Finals was a suggestion from a scouting assistant who was not even a part of Kerr's main coaching staff. He bought into the idea and even credited the man responsible for it.

And during courtside huddles, Steve Kerr's humility and openness would get him to question his players whether they saw something on the court that he does not see. Kerr understands his limitations; he is not omnipotent as a coach. He makes mistakes and might overlook an important element from time to time. That is the exact reason why he listens to his assistants and players. Leandro Barbosa recounts a time when he suggested a late-game play to Steve Kerr when the latter asked the team for suggestions. As he always did, Kerr used the play and eventually won the game.

Looking back at to Steve Kerr first met with the team, one of his first phrases was that he believed that the team could win without him. That was the mantra he had been running the team on in the three seasons he has coached the Golden State Warriors. He had them buy into his selfless system of ball and people movement. He completely put his faith and trust in players he believed could make a difference for the team.

True enough, the Warriors proved they could win without Kerr. They went half a season without him during the 2015-16 campaign but ended up losing only four games in his absence. The culture and the system had already been set in place. Even without Kerr, the Warriors can win titles and dominate the league. But, in a sense, they also need Steve Kerr.

As all-time great Ernest Hemingway once said, "The best way to find out if you can trust somebody is to trust them." There was no assurance on the part of Kerr that his team would excel if he gave them his full trust. But Kerr did it anyway. He made them believe they could win without him. But the Warriors still need Steve Kerr more than anyone thinks. They need him to be there to trust them.

Conclusion

During Steve Kerr's dramatic earlier years, he had to grow up amidst chaotic times in Beirut. The death of his father and the distance of his family had him focusing on basketball and treating his teammates with the same respect and dignity as family members. One can easily understand how Steve Kerr developed his philosophies and methodologies in basketball as a coach.

Even when he became a player under famed coaches such as Phil Jackson and Gregg Popovich in the NBA, the story remained the same. Jackson was a coach that openly communicated to his players like family. He allowed them to be themselves. That was why Michael Jordan's competitive spirit never wavered under Jackson and why Dennis Rodman remained an unorthodox personality even after winning titles with the Bulls. And for Kerr, Phil Jackson accepted him for his athletic weaknesses and used him for his smarts and his strength at shooting. It was a family based on acceptance when Kerr was with the Bulls.

It was with the San Antonio Spurs where Steve Kerr learned how much Gregg Popovich values open communication between coaches and players and how he treats everyone, from his staff all the way to the final man on the bench, as a member of a family. Pop was a father figure above being a mentor to Steve Kerr. He trusted everyone in the team and often jokes around his players to lighten the mood of an otherwise strict method of disciplining players. As with the Bulls, the Spurs were like family to Kerr because of how Pop treated them like his own.

When Steve Kerr would finally become a coach of his team, he never changed his approach in treating his players from when he was still playing under Lute Olson at the University of Arizona up to the time he retired as a Spur in 2003. Kerr allowed his players to be themselves and gave them the freedom and choice to do what they wanted to do on the hard floor.

As always, it boiled down to how much Steve Kerr trusted his players as if they were family. The freedom he gave Steph Curry to shoot what would have otherwise been ill-advised 30-footers from deep, for Klay Thompson to keep on shooting whenever he's hot, for Draymond Green to keep the intensity burning when other coaches would have tried to tame him, and for the bench to contribute in their way allowed the Golden State Warriors to in turn learn how to trust and treat their coach with utmost respect and dignity.

But no matter how much freedom and trust a coach gives his players, the most important aspect of coaching will always be the system. Steve Kerr, in line with how much freedom he gives his team, also allowed them to be free on the court by implementing a system that advocated and utilized the best ball movement in the history of basketball. There were plays made for everyone on the team because of how much ball movement they utilize night in and night out. Steve Kerr always made sure that the ball found its way to everyone on the court. In a way, he also allows the ball itself to be as free as his players are.

While it may sound simple given as how Kerr's philosophies and methodologies are more on the aspect of being himself and letting their players be themselves as well, he was also lucky enough to be given the opportunity to play under great coaches and to inherit a team that already had the right pieces. His personnel decisions are also to be lauded considering he kept around veteran and young minds alike in his staff while knowing who to keep and who to sign on his team.

With all that said and done, what any coach or aspiring coach could learn from Steve Kerr is the sense of freedom and joy of handling a team like they are a part of your family. He jokes around with his players, competes with them on a healthy basis, communicates to them what he has on his mind, and allows them to grow and evolve at their pace. On top of all that, he has maintained his humility and would rather credit his staff and his players for whatever success they see.

While others would rather be more technical, professional, and strict in their approach, Kerr's philosophy in coaching the Warriors are as free and as fluid as his offensive system is. He keeps an open mind and promotes freedom of discourse of ideas among his staff and players. He coaches like an academic professor, who also embraces his students as an extension of his family. In a way, he has grown to be so much like his grandfather and his father.

And though Kerr's approach and system may not always work with other teams and players because of the differences in personality, skills, talent level, personnel, and competition, what others may learn from his approach and philosophy is that coaching will never be about what the coach believes and what he thinks is right. Like a family, there is freedom of discourse and an opportunity to learn from everyone in the household. Steve Kerr treats his time the same way. He joined the Warriors not only to coach them to championships, but also to let them grow freely on their own. In a sense, Kerr himself also learned and grew from what he took out from his experience with his staff and his players. Coaching is a free-flowing learning process as Kerr himself shows, and that is what most coaches seem to forget as they stick to their mindset and beliefs.

Final Word/About the Author

I was born and raised in Norwalk, Connecticut. Growing up, I could often be found spending many nights watching basketball, soccer, and football matches with my father in the family living room. I love sports and everything that sports can embody. I believe that sports are one of most genuine forms of competition, heart, and determination. I write my works to learn more about influential athletes and coaches in the hopes that from my writing, you the reader can walk away inspired to put in an equal if not greater amount of hard work and perseverance to pursue your goals. If you enjoyed *Steve Kerr: The Inspiring Life and Leadership Lessons of One of Basketball's Greatest Coaches,* please leave a review! Also, you can read more of my works on *Gregg Popovich, Roger Federer, Novak Djokovic, Andrew Luck, Rob Gronkowski, Brett Favre, Calvin Johnson, Drew Brees, J.J. Watt, Colin Kaepernick, Aaron Rodgers, Peyton Manning, Tom Brady, Russell Wilson,*

Michael Jordan, LeBron James, Kyrie Irving, Klay Thompson, Stephen Curry, Kevin Durant, Russell Westbrook, Anthony Davis, Chris Paul, Blake Griffin, Kobe Bryant, Joakim Noah, Scottie Pippen, Carmelo Anthony, Kevin Love, Grant Hill, Tracy McGrady, Vince Carter, Patrick Ewing, Karl Malone, Tony Parker, Allen Iverson, Hakeem Olajuwon, Reggie Miller, Michael Carter-Williams, John Wall, James Harden, Tim Duncan, Steve Nash, Draymond Green, Kawhi Leonard, Dwyane Wade, Ray Allen, Pau Gasol, Dirk Nowitzki, Jimmy Butler, Paul Pierce, Manu Ginobili, Pete Maravich, Larry Bird, Kyle Lowry, Jason Kidd, David Robinson, LaMarcus Aldridge, Derrick Rose, Paul George, Kevin Garnett, Chris Paul, Marc Gasol, Yao Ming, Al Horford, Amar'e Stoudemire, DeMar DeRozan, Isaiah Thomas, Kemba Walker and Chris Bosh in the Kindle Store. If you love basketball, check out my website at claytongeoffreys.com to join my exclusive list where I let you know about my latest books and give you lots of goodies.

Like what you read? Please leave a review!

I write because I love sharing the stories of influential coaches like Steve Kerr with fantastic readers like you. My readers inspire me to write more so please do not hesitate to let me know what you thought by leaving a review! If you love books on life, basketball, or productivity, check out my website at claytongeoffreys.com to join my exclusive list where I let you know about my latest books. Aside from being the first to hear about my latest releases, you can also download a free copy of *33 Life Lessons: Success Principles, Career Advice & Habits of Successful People*. See you there!

Clayton

References

[i] "Steve Kerr Bio". *NBA.com*. Web

[ii] Branch, John. "Tragedy Made Steve Kerr See the World Beyond the Court". *New York Times*. 22 December 2016. Web

[iii] Wilner, Jon. "Warriors Coach Steve Kerr Guided By His Father's Life and Lessons". *Mercury News*. 18 May 2015. Web

[iv] Korman, Chris. "The Assassination of Steve Kerr's Father and the Unlikely Story Of A Champion". *USA Today*. 3 June 2015. Web

[v] Smith, Sam. "Steve Kerr's Unlikely Journey". *NBA.com*. Web

[vi] Smith, Sam. "Kerr Employing Jackson's Philosophy with Warriors". *Japan Times*. 14 April 2015. Web

[vii] Saunders, Dusty. "A Blow to Broadcasting: Steve Kerr". *Denver Post*. 11 May 2014. Web.

[viii] "Steve Kerr Becomes Fastest Coach to 200 Wins in Professional Sports History". *NBA.com*. 28 March 2017. Web

[ix] Smith, Sam. "Steve Kerr Leads With Unique Style". *NBA.com*. 6 December 2014. Web

[x] Bourne, Jacob. "Gregg Popovich Says It Was 'Easy to See' Steve Kerr Would Become Coach". *Bleacher Report*. 12 November 2014. Web

[xi] Ballard, Chris. "Why Steph Curry and Steve Kerr Are Among the World's Greatest Leaders". *Fortune*. 25 May 2016. Web

[xii] Kroichick, Ron. "Humility Goes a Long Way For Steve Kerr in Title Run". *San Francisco Chronicle*. 18 June 2015. Web

[xiii] Berman, Marc. "How Steve Kerr Keeps David Lee Happy – While Planted on the Bench". *New York Post*. 4 June 2015. Web

[xiv] Ballard, Chris. "Warriors: From One-Dimensional and One-And-Done to NBA Title Favorites". *Sports Illustrated*. 19 February 2015. Web

[xv] Yaeger, Don. "Dynamic Leadership: Steve Kerr's Secret for Coaching Success". *Forbes*. 24 August 2015. Web

[xvi] Davis, Scott. "Warriors Coach Reveals Team Philosophy That Helps Make Stephen Curry So Dangerous". *Business Insider*. 8 March 2016. Web

[xvii] Ostler, Scott. "Steve Kerr's Rhythm And Flow Offense

Synthesized From Triangle, Popovich, D'Antoni". *San Francisco Chronicle*. 5 June 2016. Web

[xviii] Strauss, Ethan. "How the Warriors Built the NBA's Top Defense". *ESPN*. 4 February 2015. Web

Made in the USA
Las Vegas, NV
30 September 2021